Poet's England – 21
Derbyshire

Poet's England – 21
Derbyshire

Compiled and Edited

by

Alison Chisholm

Illustrated by HOWARD COLES

HEADLAND

First published in 1999
by
HEADLAND PUBLICATIONS
38 York Avenue, West Kirby,
Wirral. CH48 3JF

A full CIP record for this book is available
from the British Library

ISBN 1 902096 45 2

HEADLAND acknowledges the financial
assistance of North West Arts Board

Printed in Great Britain by
L. Cocker & Co., Berry Street, Liverpool

CONTENTS

3

DERBYSHIRE

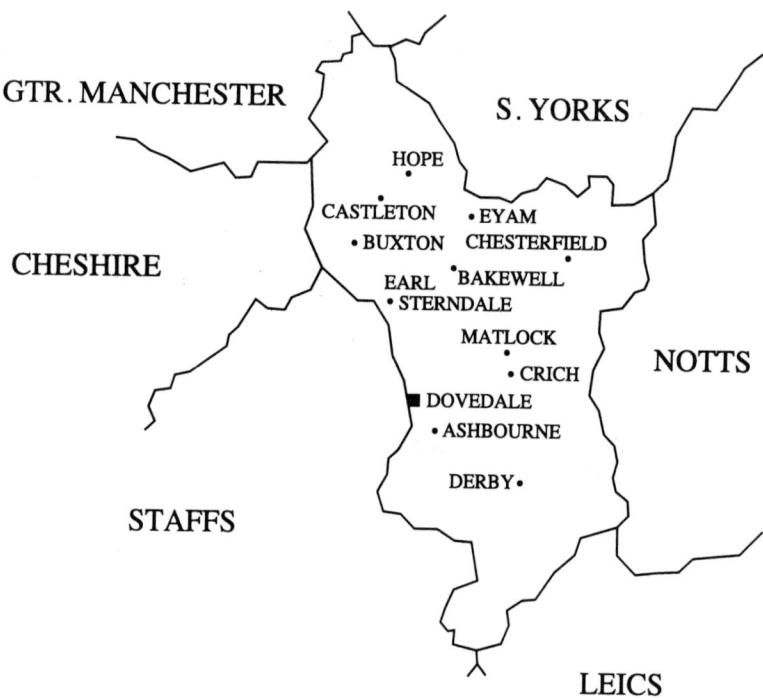

GTR. MANCHESTER

S. YORKS

CHESHIRE

HOPE

CASTLETON
BUXTON

EYAM
CHESTERFIELD

EARL
STERNDALE

BAKEWELL

MATLOCK

CRICH

NOTTS

DOVEDALE
ASHBOURNE

DERBY

STAFFS

LEICS

FOREWORD

Situated in the centre of England, Derbyshire draws together the most exciting elements from all corners of the country. The county is full of contrasts; bustling towns and isolated farms, moorland and woodland, craggy rocks and lush river valleys, the pleasure gardens of Matlock Bath and the elegance of Buxton. The visitor can enjoy walking in the Peak District National Park (Britain's first National Park) exploring underground caverns where the unique bluejohn stone is found, travelling on a tram at the National Tramway Museum, discovering the treasures of a stately home such as Chatsworth House or Haddon Hall, trying to fathom the mysteries of the stone circle at Arbor Low, or learning the history of Eyam, the 'plague village'.

In years gone by, Derbyshire has not produced as many great literary figures as some other counties, such as Cumbria: but Charles Cotton, William Wordsworth, Henry Alford and Anna Seward have all been inspired to write about this part of the country.The varied facets of the county have prompted today's poets to produce a rich seam of writing. Local customs and characters have provided an equally fertile source. There are poems about the delightful well dressing ceremonies, the Bakewell puddings (NOT to be confused with the vastly inferior Bakewell tarts), Mrs. Hancock, whose family was decimated in the Eyam plague epidemic, and Chattering Charteris, the gossip who was silenced for ever. There is humour and tragedy, pain and joy — the whole tapestry of life woven in poetry.

The collection begins with a broad view of Derbyshire, and then travels through Buxton, Eyam, Bakewell, Dovedale, Ashbourne, Derby and Matlock, taking in rivers, dales, mountains and caves, characters, customs and villages on its way.

Selecting the pieces to include here has been an exhilarating task. I am indebted to Guy Stapleton for his generous help, and to the poets of the past and present for their wonderful work which celebrates the life, people, culture, history, geography, geology, legend and folklore of Derbyshire. I hope that reading this collection enthralls you as much as compiling it fascinated me.

Alison Chisholm

Hardwick Hall

SEVEN WONDERS

Ancient Chatsworth stood assault
Siege and storm and thunderbolt:
Workmen then with beef and brawn
Came and pulled it stone from stone.

Mam Tor that shivers indeed
Suffers frost that picks its load,
Winter winds from moor and field
And the moon that shines so cold.

Ebb and Flow at Barmoor Clough
First made farmers frown and laugh
Then by savants was discussed:
All that sorcery stopped at last.

Bearded Leicester, boots and cape,
Watched them drop a lusty, hale
Stalwart into Elden Hole:
Crazed he came up on the rope.

Peak Cavern at Castleton
Frightened men of flesh and bone:
Candles might where none had trod
Light some netherworld abode.

Roofed against both shower and sun
St. Ann's Well, anciently known,
Unites springs tepid and cold:
Sickness is cured and pain lulled.

Last of all there is Poole's Cave
Which for Cotton's sake please love:
Of its rareties he the sum
First wrote down that's still the same.

Edward Boaden Thomas

SONNET XLIX

Long have we toiled, and passed from day to day
Our stated round of duties, till the mind
Reaches for change, and longs fresh paths to find
From her accustomed dwelling far away:
Come, then, dear wife, while yet the summer ray
Fills all the air with gladness, and unbind
Awhile the chains of duty; then reclined
Where Derwent or where Dove in varied play
Leaps through his mossy rocks, let us entice
The wary trout, or ply the pencil's art;
Or in some wooded dell that lies apart
Woo the maid Poesy: no unworthy price
Of year—long labour without ceasing wrought,
And intermission of poetic thought.

Henry Alford (1810-1871)

BC

My family's bones lie in this land.
A thigh bone bared at Cresswell Crags
high in a cave of hewn lime rock
hid by time in a fern-sprayed crack.

By Unston, Dunston, Appeknowle and Brushes
my mesolithic mother carved tusk to make
needle, pick, hair-comb, skin-scrape,
her carbonised grain pot and bone rake.

My Brigante father cracked roman skulls,
forayed from his fort at Mam Tor
on cattle raids. He marked out the best
and fattest beast from the valley floor.

My brother's horse threw a splint
as he galloped hard on Rykneild Street
hobbled, ambushed by Caesar's legions —
left crossroad swinging by his feet.

My sister of the Beaker People
chipped flint flakes, boiled up woad.
Bleached to white she lies in a barrow
by the ley lines of Arbor Low.

My family's bones are scattered here
from Chesterfield to Cromford Rocks,
bits of Allen, Hayes and Fletcher —
I hear their whisper from hill and loch.

Judith Thwaite

DERBYSHIRE MEN

"I' Darbyshire who're born an' bred,
Are strong i' th' arm, bu' weak i' th' head":
    So th' lying Proverb says.
Strength o' th' arm. who doubts shall feel:
Strength o' th' head, its power can seal
    The lips that scoff, always.

The rich vein'd Mine, the Mountain hoar,
We sink, an' blast, an' pierce, 'an bore
    By th' might o' Darby brawn.
An' Darby brain con think an' plon,
As well as that o' ony mon;
    An' clearly as the morn.

"Strong i' th' arm, an' strong i' th' head,"
The fou' fause Proverb should ha' said,
    If th' truth she meant to tell.
Bu' th' union, so wise an' rare
O *brawn an' brain,* she didna care
    To see or speak of well.

The jealous jade, nor Darby born,
Where praise wor due, pour'd forth bu' scorn,
    An' lying words let fau.
Bu' far above the Proverb stands
The Truth, that God's Almighty hands
Ha' welded strength an' mind i' one;
An' pour'd it down i' plenty on
    Born Darbyshire men au.

Walter Kirkland (1864)

12

MONUMENTS TO UNKNOWN MEN

I wonder if they thought of rural hikes,
where watchful walkers view the brindled quilts
on centuries of bleakest acres, glad
with the beauty of chuckling streams. Or spring

encounters : spotty lambs and ragbag ewes,
the flopping peewits, constant crows, and winds
that shake and fidget through these solemn stacks,
each boundary a belt of trusted rocks.

All a million chunky stones a mile
of no particular state or stature,
though tie-stones maybe longer, thin or flat.
Each single stone was chosen by a man,

who lent and picked it from the ground and placed
it gently on the one before, such skill.
And each side leaned towards the other as
it gained in height; its grandeur matched his will.

The cavities and myriad crannies, homes
for countless life, are vital as the walls
themselves that portion up the land. Yet those
who built it maybe couldn't write their name.

Before the walls was open space, not fields.
These demarcations kept the flocks within.
They symbolized an ownership, a plot,
a territory, unit wage, or debt.

Memorials to toiling hands and men
of skill endure; define the lives and plight
of families, so modest and resigned,
and so retain the nature of this land.

But centuries of wildest wear and tear
are proof, and justice to the claim that men
of simple means do make their mark, enrich
this land of hope and doubt yet die unknown.

Brian Blackwell

WHITE PEAK SPRING

Between Ilam, Youlgreave and Alstonefield
   high pasture lies, a billowing quilt
      white-sewn with dry-stone walls.

Over Thorpe Cloud, Arbor Low, Parsley Hey,
   lark-song cascades over calling lambs
      to staccato mock of cuckoo.

Through Dovedale and Lathkill Dale
   running base of ribbling river,
      trout in rock pools, wagtails, dippers.

In Hartington and Tissington
   gilley-flowers spatter lime-grey houses,
      petals reflect old stories at the wells.

By Mill Dale and Miller's Dale
   cliffs and crags grow bluebells at their feet,
      yellow catkins curtain the caves.

Between Buxton, Ashbourne and Matlock Bath
   high pasture lies a billowing quilt
      white-sewn with dry-stone walls.

Mary Brett

IN DERBYSHIRE

In Derbyshire
They go in for scenery
In small doses.
For instance,
You can be walking along
A perfectly ordinary road
When suddenly,
There —
There between the houses,
Or two factories,
Or between the mill shop and the garage,
In miniature,
A microcosm of the English countryside,
An eighteenth century watercolour.
Or in the evening, silhouetted —
Nothing elaborate you understand,
No ostentation, no vulgar flamboyance —
Just a few trees,
Self-conscious hill,
A cowherd and his dog.
    Perfection.

Elsie M. Torrent

DRY STONE WALLS

A touch of comfort on bare hills
scorings from the past
where the wild allows
indifferently
a small attachment
to humanity.

Gleaming wet in groping fog
black beneath the sun
they climb high
as hope in early manhood.
Blundering, bewildered sheep
crumble them in places
and razor winds
seek any lack of balance.

They never tame the moorland
yet from their careful building
stone on patient stone
man himself may reach
the misted peaks.

Peggy Poole

SCENES THROUGH A LONG LENS

Chatsworth

glimpsed between dark trees
deer flashing arcs of rust red
imprint memory

Derwent

needles of sunlight
exploding in reflection
stab the watching eye

Youlgreave

campfire doused by rain
fingers raw from dixie scrub
ging-gang sing-song blues

North Wingfield

cow looks gently down
dead cow lies with belly split
white floor running blood

Matlock

uncle's motorbike
cousins squashed in the sidecar
delicious day out

Bakewell Show

banks in caravans
rosettes on prize-winning cows
striped tent migraine

Dethick

farmer tossed by bull
pillow eaten by pony
another damp camp

Brimington

> ghost station ghost rails
> games at a godparents' house
> cartwheels on the lawn

Dove Dale

> slippy stepping stones
> beige handbag floating downstream
> lady's hysterics

Eyam

> in the parish church
> reading register of deaths
> timeless empathy

Chesterfield

> shaded eyes see spire
> twisted in imperfection
> but celebrated

Bakewell

> grandma in teashop
> delectable confection
> spoilt children again

Castleton

> drip stalactite drip
> plastic comb in plastic case
> stalag souvenir

Buxton

> pillion novice
> clutching uncle's leather waist
> good vibrations

Monsal Dale

> trains run viaduct
> deep green river valley song
> bridge to yesterday

Hilary Tinsley

HAREBELL ON LOSE HILL

I stayed again with friends in Hope.

In the morning under scudding sky
we three set out to climb Lose Hill,
and all the way I was aware
you were not here completing symmetry,
casting a fourth shadow,
integral corner of a square.

We climbed by stone walls into wind's teeth
bowing before its brunt,
scaling the ridge where solitary farm
huddles beneath slant trees;
short wiry grasses quivered, sprung,
and under every wall the harebell hung.

Harebell, colour of ever-present intangible distance,
fragile in close-up as time is brief,
and, as I learned that evening,
symbol of grief.

Mary Hodgson

KINDER SCOUT

Laughter, the joy of youth, anticipation,
Forward looking to the thrill of climb.
Not mountaineering, but steady upward progress,
Harmony bursting on all senses
Eyes excited, bird song lifts —
Hands touch, grass smells green — pure water
On the pulse of Kinder.

Kindred minds, love surges through such friendship
Beyond the outward signs, words scarce define.
When darkening clouds spill out their distant warnings
Those unseen threads hold strong
Together — binds the common aim.
Encouraging each other
Though mists descend, shrouding senses
There is still the call of Kinder.

Fears also shared, although perhaps unspoken
Each silenced, contained within some deep recess.
Familiar signs now hidden, each step uncertain
Still a song is borne though hollow sounding
Urging onward, still as one
Longing for a guide, some sign
To lead us over Kinder.

Immortal print of one who went before us
Within the mud embedded — observed by downcast eyes,
Identified by anxious searching travellers
Guiding step by step some young and weary hopefuls
Leading onward though unseen
Skirting danger. You never knew we followed, when
You lead us over Kinder.

Elizabeth Mansfield

THE LADYBOWER
(opened by King George VI, 1945)

Filled by the River Derwent,
the man-made lake extends
dissembling as a Scottish loch
land-locked among conifers;
no piper's skirl is heard
scouring this heather-glen.

The thin pipe of water-fowl,
of the shy willow warbler
probing the upland scrub,
might just barely disturb
the angler's concentration
sifting the morning mists.

Day hikers heading
for Bleaklow or Featherbed Top
edging the Pennine Way
are drawn to this ceaseless water,
to the clear ring of hills,
to some fine inns it spawned.

J.D.Mallinson

UNDER LADYBOWER

*(Two villages were drowned when
Ladybower Reservoir was created in 1943)*

In time of drought the village reappears,
Slowly at first, with broken roofs and walls,
Like little islands, dotted here and there;
Half-hidden reefs. Then, as the level falls,
Outlines are clearer, gardens are revealed,
Traces of road, lost field and stunted hedge,
All the small details that have been concealed
Like shameful secrets. Here among the sedge
Was there a garden border, bright with blooms?
Across the falling lake, is that the keep
Of some old castle with a hundred rooms,
Like Beauty, sent to an untimely sleep?

Today the displaced villagers descend
To walk, nostalgic, on the cracking clay,
Searching for small reminders of the day
They left their homes some fifty years ago.
This one recalls an orchard rich with pears,
Another points to where the plums would fall.
It was the same for everyone, they say.
Even the Squire was made to leave the Hall.

But when the waters rise and close again
Above the roofless cottages and barns,
Do antique waggons rumble by with grain
Past inns where ancients sit and tell their yarns?
Do birds and fishes dart among the trees
And in the spireless church, do choirs still sing?
Are there still clovered meadows for the bees
And, though the bells are gone, do they still ring?

Sometimes I think I see the beams of light
Cast by the daimlers on the laurel drive
Or, from an earlier age, the swinging rays
Of carriage lanterns guiding laughing guests
Towards the music and the revelry.
And when at last I turn away my gaze
Do those departed dancers meet again
For polka, minuet or saraband?
Only the moorhen and the mallard know
What ghostly figures haunt the depths below.

Beryl Lewin

PEAK CAVERN

The chattering jackdaws haunt the cavemouth still;
    Their cries re-echo round the high rockface,
    And sounds of dripping water fill this place,
Beneath the castle ruins on the hill.

And twenty years ago it was the same,
    In summertime, so cool and greenly dim,
    The chattering daws protested at our whim
To savour and explore the cavern's fame.

And centuries ago, did jackdaws cry,
    When Peveril Castle reared up strong and new?
    And did those Normans see with wonder too
This mighty cave and cliff that reached the sky?

And, ages since, what creatures had their lair
    Within this cave, which tried their quarry sore
    Who made their ancient camp up on Mam Tor,
The Shivering Mountain slowly crumbling there?

And now — dank valley, with a bubbling stream,
    And hoary, moss-grown rock, tremendous, old,
    And mighty cave, mysterious, marvellous, cold,
Hold close their secrets, far from sunlight's gleam.

Pat Moneypenny

WINNATS PASS

Three of us struggled out of appalling nightmares —
the kind that still stay with you when you wake,
screaming.

Yet we were warm and safe inside our camping van.
We'd had a glorious day basking in the first
summer sunshine trapped in that narrow valley.

We'd explored a cave, the children gatthering
Blue John halfway up the hill — the cave was spacious
but the entrance small, half hidden. We fancied
no one knew that it was there.

Later that day the farmer told us all about
the couple on their honeymoon, many years ago,
shot for their money, their bodies stuffed
inside a cave — *our* cave.

Margaret Caunt

GIFT FROM BLUE JOHN

Steps took me from air,
sunlight and heather
deprived me of hill and dale
and comfortable sheep.

Darkness closed in,
echoed with the guide's voice
offering information for minds
too subdued to be receptive.

I panic underground,
prefer rivers, mountains,
and struggle to control fear
as steps, slippery and eroded,
went down and down and down
until they came at last
into an arena where
in artificial light
stalactites shone.

But on that long descent
in a niche of grim rock-face,
denied light and warmth,
young green bracken grew
owing its birth perhaps
to some unsuspecting tourist.

Blue John is the only cavern
I have ever explored
and over passing years
those leaves have taken root
in my mind; they
colour my darkness,
have become a touchstone.

Peggy Poole

THE LEGEND OF LOVER'S LEAP

They watched, it is said, amazed
As the maid in her crinoline,
Crazed by the jilting, ran —
Scorning bramble and thorn
That tried to claw her back —
To the top of the crag, where she stood
Her legs coursing with blood.

They watched, it is said, in awe
The fleetness of her rise,
The grimness of her face,
The branding of her glare,
And watched, it is said, in fear
As she stepped onto the air.

One neat little blood-bright foot,
And before the crowd had groaned,
Its pair.

Her crying-out stopped hearts
A hundred miles away,
Three million years ago,
The age before yesterday.
And in the years to be
When a climber in Lycra tights
Would shudder at his stance
As a froth of petticoat frill
Issued from the clouds.

Sharks that ghost the gorge
Marvel at how it was:
How the villagers shut their eyes
To the moment of the smash.
But thinking of the falling slow
Again to heaven inclined,
Watched, it is said, amazed
A blackening of the sky,
The gentle downward float
Of a billowing silk-gilled dress,
Two slender blooded legs;
Her forgiving face.

Frances Nagle

BUXTON IN A RAINY SEASON

From these wild heights, where oft the mists descend
In rains that shroud the sun and chill the gale,
Each transient gleaming interval we hail,
And rock the naked valleys, and extend
Our gaze around where yon vast mountains blend
With billowy clouds that o'er their summits sail,
Pondering how little Nature's charms befriend
The barren scene, monotonous and pale.
Yet solemn when the darkening shadows fleet
Successive o'er the wide and silent hills,
Gilded by watery sunbeams; then we meet
Peculiar pomp of vision. Fancy thrills;
And owns there is no scene so rude and bare
But nature sheds or grace or grandeur there.

Anna Seward (1780)

BUXTON

Epigram

Buxton, whose fame thy milk-warm waters tell,
Whom I, perhaps, no more shall see, farewell!

Mary, Queen of Scots (1542-1587)

BUXTON RITUAL

The pattern never changed. One hovered
on double yellows while market crowd pressed,
the other queued in steam and grease,
and children ran between us
communicating 'lots of salt'
or 'breadcrumbs, not batter.' Then
the short drive downhill
— grey roads, grey houses —
to park where lake and trees
made an acute angle.

Ambrosia was whitest flakes of haddock,
vinegar and onions, gold slicked chips;
and grease marks on the new Dick Francis
never mattered. Hot and sated,
we stumbled from the car with scraps;
and ducks and geese, swans, pigeons
rode a tide toward us.

Across the stream swings beckoned,
rides to make the day a party; blue
pool water enticed. At the Pavilion's core
we prowled gift shops, bought lemon cheese
or shoebags from the WI, chose ices.

Conservatory, Opera House, Victorian letter box —
we counted off each landmark
willing them to be there, fearing change.

Years away, I cannot remember
when the chain was broken — wonder
if I should have heeded warnings
in those ritual snapshots,
seen the woman gleam
in little girls' eyes. Perhaps the pool
still laps, the river flows,
they still serve chips in the market place.

These days we travel by a different route.

Alison Chisholm

MRS WILLOUGHBY'S KISS
(For Buxton Opera House)

A kiss. A kiss. A kiss. This stage
rages on while warm hearts beat.
What then? That cherub there,
on that proscenium arch,
he bangs his tambourine.
He'd have them come again —
those names —
He'd raise their skeletons. He would.

The pulse of this place urges on:
love, hate, virtue, pain,
treading the boards.
Once a fire came close, but did not dare.
They say a flame of Edmund Kean
rose in the air.
His bones creaked through the door.

His breath, the morning light,
sang out litanies of love,
bristling on the moor's chest,
whistling through dry stone walls.
This mad play called *Theatre*,
though it were stabbed to death,
would always rise again.

Wendy Bardsley

*(Mrs Willoughby's Kiss is the title of the play performed
at the opening of the Opera House, Monday 1st June
1903).*

BUXTON SPA

A jar of Buxton
Spa   water
on a   warm day
is   true   bliss
if gurgle-gottled
and   gotten
from   a   bottle;
and if my lips don't
have   to   kiss
an   ancient   cold   tap
in   the   Crescent
when I   hastily
queue   knowing
I'll   dislike
the   taste   of
the   waters
springing   from
there ....

Arda Lacey

POOLE'S CAVERN

(from Wonders of the Peake)

Through a blind door (which some poor woman there
Still keeps the key of, that it may keep her)
Men bowing low take leave of day's fair light,
To crowd themselves into the womb of the night,
Through such a low and narrow pass, that it
For badgers, wolves, and foxes seems more fit;
Or for the less sorts of chaces, then
T'admit the statures, and the bulks of men,
Could it to reason any way appear
That men could find out any business there.

But having fifteen paces crept or more,
Through pointed stones and dirt upon all four,
The gloomy grotto lets men upright rise
Although they were six times Goliath's size.
There, looking upward, your astonish'd sight
Beholds the glory of the sparkling light
Th'enamel'd roof darts round about the place,
With so subduing but ingrateful rays
As to put out the lights, by which alone
They receive lustre, that before had none,
And must to darkness be resign'd when they are gone.

But here a roaring torrent bids you stand,
Fording you climb a rock on the right hand,
Which hanging, pent-house-like, does overlook
The dreadful channel of the rapid brook,
So deep, and black, the very thought does make
My brains turn giddy and my eye-balls ake.
Over this dangerous precipice you crawl,
Lost if you slip, for if you slip you fall;
But whither, faith 'tis no great matter, when
Y'are sure ne'er to be seen alive agen.

Propt round with peasants, on you trembling go,
Whilst, every step you take, your guides do show
In the uneven rock the uncouth shapes
Of men, of lions, horses, dogs, and apes:
But so resembling each the fancied shape,
The man might be the horse, the dog the ape.
And straight just in your way a stone appears
Which the resemblance of a hay-cock bears
Some four foot high, and beyond that a less
Of the same figure; which do still increase
In height, and bulk, by a continual drop,
Which upon each distilling from the top,
And falling still exactly on the crown,
There break themselves to mists, which trickling down
Crust into stone, and (but with leisure) swell
The sides, and still advance the miracle.
So that in time, they would be tall enough,
If they were need, to prop the hanging roof,
Did not sometimes the curious visitors
To stead a treasure is not justly theirs,
Break off much more at one injurious blow
Than can again in many ages grow.

Charles Cotton (c 1675)

MILLERS DALE

Barefoot we went by Millers Dale
When meadowsweet was golden gloom
And happy love was in the vale
Singing upon the summer bloom
Of gypsy-crop and branches laid
Of willows over chanting pools,
Barefoot by Millers Dale we made
Our summer festival of fools.

Folly bright-eyed, and quick, and young
Was there with all his silly plots,
And trotty wagtail stepped among
The delicate forget-me-nots,
And laughter played with us above
The rocky shelves and weeded holes,
And we had fellowship to love
The pigeon and the water-voles.

Time soon shall be when we are all
Stiller than ever runs the Wye,
And every bitterness shall fall
Tomorrow in obscurity,
And wars be done, and treasons fail,
Yet shall new friends go down to greet
The singing rocks of Millers Dale,
And willow pools and meadowsweet.

1916   *John Drinkwater (1882-1937)*

MILLER'S DALE

No passengers standing
on the stone platform overgrown
with bleached grass. Toddlers
crawl through the picnics spread
between striped deckchairs.

And the banks of the railway trail
are so thick with knapweed, clover,
stitchwort, purple vetch,
I catch my child self
gleaning sparser hedgerows,

my mother telling me flowers,
names. When the sun is heavy
on my back I sit on a log
out of its reach. Tree
heads fill the ravine,

hide the river chattering
below. I find a flower
with a cup of white petals,
nod at hikers. Insects
flicker across the quiet.

The gorge widens, reveals
through beech and willow foliage:
a mill chimney, caving
walls, window sockets,
torn doors. Somewhere:

water churning wildly.
A couple on bikes pedal by,
each ferrying a child
with browned, sturdy thighs.
But I've read the plaque by the path,

am staring at Devil's Mill
where seven-year-olds
shut from summer, shuffled
among the cotton-spinning machines
till their thin legs buckled.

Myra Schneider

REMEMBER EYAM

Today I visited the orchard graves
Where years ago I laid my sons to rest,
The churchyard being full.
Beneath the blossom of the apple-trees
I wondered if it had been for the best
And was it all God's will?

The carter brought a city pestilence
In garments coiled like adders in a box
Awaiting their release.
So all that month we hid ourselves indoors
While, skulking like a fox,
Crept the disease.

Soon every household had its agony,
But when we sought to pack our goods and flee
The Rector bade us stay,
Begging us not to risk our neighbours' lives.
And so reluctantly we heard his plea;
There seemed no other way.

For dread of passing on the fatal germ
We could not gather in the church to pray,
So met in Cucklet Dell.
We sang our hymns beneath the open sky,
Fearfully wondering for whose poor clay
Would toll the mourning bell.

How hard it was to see the little birds
Fly freely to and fro while we stayed here
Watching our children die,
Dipping our coins in vinegar to pay
For food the neighbours brought to us in fear.
We could not even cry.

Remember, strangers, when you see the mounds
In churchyard, field and orchard, all grown green,
Had we not held so firm
The whole of England might have felt that clutch
Of creeping death, and your forebears had been
As fodder for the worm.

And so we sacrificed our hopes of joy
And stayed imprisoned until terror ceased
For what appeared a dream.
O distant visitors, spare a moment's thought,
Remembering that a few of you at least
May owe your lives to Eyam.

Beryl Lewin

WAITING

I am the stone
where the coins were thrown
at Eyam.
I am the grass
that grows round the stone
where coins were thrown
by shaking hands
at Eyam.
I am the soil
that roots the grass
that winds the stone
where the coins were thrown
that kept alive
the fearful eyes
at Eyam.
I am the stone.

Maggie Norton

MRS HANCOCK'S DILEMMA
IN A THEOLOGICAL AGE

(Her husband and six children died of the Plague
within a few days of each other.)

Anne was the last to go.
I gave no tears, no sorrow,
only a promise to follow
which I could not keep.
Now, unlike mine, their sleep
is unbroken; together they make
towards Heaven while I keep wake
alone in my bed, aware of the hollow
beside me, the hollow within.

In desperate fear I tread thin
tightrope of grief; unrestrained,
it would seem I arraign
the Almighty in Heaven above —
yet too pinched control
plays false those dear ones,
makes ingrate my soul.
Either way whelms me in sin,
leads thus to a final parting.

Oh monstrous! He whose whim
can seven times toll the knell
to take my loves to Him,
plunge me in Hell.

Mary Hodgson

38

THE 200TH VICTIM
from the Parish Register of Eyam Church:
"1666. August 25th. Katherine Mompesson."

The village wrapped its poisonous cloak
closely round itself, forcing
the festering sores to ooze within.
A desolate dance with death
performed alone, apart, for love
of those who lived beyond the hills.

Burials were swift: no prayers
no tolling bell; each Sunday
fewer climbed the steep
green slopes of Cucklet Delph
to gather underneath the cragged arch.

Later that August day
walking in sun-soaked fields
Katherine took her husband's hand;
she marvelled at the sweetness of the air
surely these days of dying must be done?

Above her head a curlew cried.
Today high on those hills
seven headstones tell
one family's sorrow to the winds,
while in the churchyard
Katherine's tomb
stands by the Saxon Cross.

Peggy Poole

CHATSWORTH
from The Wonders of the Peak

Southward from hence ten miles, where Derwent laves
His broken shores with never-clearing waves,
There stands a stately and stupendous pile,
Like the proud regent of the British isle,
Shedding her beams over the barren vale,
Which else bleak winds and nipping frosts assail
With such perpetual war, there would appear
Nothing but winter ten months of the year.

1681   *Charles Cotton (1630-1687)*

CHATSWORTH
On the Duke of Devonshire's Seat in Derbyshire

When Scotland's Queen, her native realms expell'd
In ancient Chatsworth was a captive held,
Had then the pile in its new charms arriv'd
Happier the captive than the Queen had liv'd!
What sighs in pity of her state could rise
That found the fugitive in paradise!

1737   *Anon*

FROM PEAK TO PALACE

Where four counties lie outspread
the gentle river Derwent takes its rise,
on windswept, dusky limestone height,
grey solitude where crying plovers
make complaining lost-soul flight
and wild and wandering things their home
on rich brown velvet of the moors.

Stream, ripples, singing, chuckling
through waving fern to pleasant valleys,
sidling past mossy impediment, hurrying
beneath dwarf tree, gnarled branching root.

Thread of dancing light, wandering
from mountain fastness, snug sheltering
nooks, blank solitudes, kind and frightening
savage and mild. The Derwent dreams
through fat meadows, by overhanging woods
and grassy slopes to Chatsworth,
moodily skirting its ornamental bridge, reflecting
Palladian frontages, grazing deer — and other herds —
the human kind, wandering, wondering
at its treasures — then tumbles
in occasional cascade, calmly journeying
through quiet broads of Darley Dale,
to join impetuous waters of the Wye.

Marie Murray

CHATSWORTH

Monuments, bridges, gardens, urns,
cascading water fountains,
visitors tinkling through
four seasons of wide gates,
wintry white fantasies,
flowers of awakening Spring,
pastel petals of still Summer
Indian Autumn fruits,
ornate decorations
inhabiting a warm marble mansion,
nestling into Derbyshire countryside,
generations of changing images.

Linda S. Hardy

THE ROCK

Night climbs the slippery sky
somewhere near Bakewell.
Humped like grazing sheep, green grey,
grey brown, hills wait,
already in the distance lose their way.

Outcrops of rain scupper the rock,
pitch into my back when I lie
face down, lost in the ill defined
hills. Flowers stop up cracks; wind bossed,
birds flutter my mind.

Under the blackening sky
This rock bears a million silences.
Its weight of birthdays dignifies my slack
red raincoat, the beat of my heart.
Strengthens me to find a way back.

Look, say the voices of silence,
'Darkness has its own map.'
As night caps the waterlogged air, once again
I stand to watch the lights from Bakewell bloom
like flowers in the rain.

Susan Skinner

OLD BAKEWELL BRIDGE

On a road leading down near a Derbyshire wood
Since the year 1300 an old bridge has stood.
Built from different shaped blocks of a rough mellow stone,
Which were hewn from the earth by a man's strength alone
They were cunningly fitted and locked into place,
Giving simple lines flowing with beauty and grace.

Rising up from the mud of the deep river bed,
There are five Gothic arches support overhead.
And suspended like diamonds, fine droplets all gleam
Where the spiders have webbed in each cranny and seam.
As the day turns to evening and shadows grow long,
Then the still air grows sweet with the nightingale's song.

And the ancient bridge glows with a rich mellow tone
As the sinking sun gently caresses the stone.
Soon the twilight falls softly, the first stars appear
And the bells from All Saint's call the people to prayer.
All alone in the darkness the old bridge will stand,
When night's black velvet cloak is enfolding the land.

Yvonne Charles

BAKEWELL PUDDING

Do not confuse me with a Bakewell tart,
that relative of mine who's sometimes laced
with pastry strips, or cherry topped and iced,
but lacks the knowledge of my baker's art.

My pedigree's immaculate, a chance
mishap in mixing by a flustered cook
who made a strawberry pie, but rushing took
a wrong ingredient without a glance

or second look and little knew she'd made
a magic mixture which would bring us fame.
Who owns that recipe? Three bakers claim
their right to it, and so their right to trade.

I only claim that those who eat me savour
the excellence of light puff pastry, race
with relish through my jammy custard base,
lick sticky fingers, thank me for my flavour.

Jean Stanbury

45

THROUGH DARK DOORS

Slowly up the steep way —
A courtyard full of yellow roses
climbing, tumbling round the doorway.
The door, massive, weighty, old,

swings open to the Medieval Hall.
Fire on the wide hearth — dead.
Huge logs, half burned, grey ash
lifts as the cold air enters with me.

In the corner an oak door,
age-worn; wrought hinges
curlecue across the ancient planks.
I push open the door and stand

on the hollow threshold of the Great Hall.
As I cross to the corner a soft soot-fall
spills across the hearth,
gentles the loneliness of my footsteps.

I know this studded door in the corner,
the wooden bar lifts easily:
worn stones, smoke-blackened beams,
comfortless hearth, but a shaft of sunlight

through the high window picks out
the balustrade of the Minstrels' Gallery.
A thread of spider-web drifts across my face,
my footsteps drag across the bare flags.

So old, the wood seems fossilised.
I run a finger down the cracks,
stand and listen to the silence
singing in my head

and I push open the door.

Berenice Moore

HADDON HALL

Romantic Haddon, built in mellow stone,
    With mullioned windows by a garden fair,
Enfolds the dream another age has known,
    That modern dreamers may, remotely, share.

The cobbled courtyard with uneven slope,
    The ante-room with curved and well-worn stair,
The great long gallery where, high in hope,
    Fair Dorothy would dance in candles' flare.

The private door that to the garden leads,
    Where quietly she slipped away unseen
To join her lover by the river meads,
    And ride with him to distant Gretna Green.

So tranquil now the long and stately room
    That echoed to that music long ago;
And tranquil too in panelled chambers' gloom,
    The past that these old vibrant houses know.

Pat Moneypenny

LATHKILL DALE

The name of that dear place
beloved these dozen years
and more
dropped
like a jewel
in the midst of the conversation

Gone the crowded cafe
the coffee cups
the cheap crockery
Gone my companions ...

Lathkill Dale ...

The day is
Whit Monday
The sun
gifts
with golden splendour
the brilliance of
massed kingcups

Here and there
an azure harebell
jingles gently
on its
slender stem

A whisper of breeze
dances. the leaves
of ash, birch
and lizard-green lime

The river is dappled
with light
yet
on the bank
where trees reach out their sheltering arms
blacker than a
raven's wing
A dark shape
skims into view

a sudden turn
and he is gone
lost in the swaying weeds
But another is there
and another
swimming slowly
gracefully
then darting across
like a
skater on ice

The water
is breathtakingly clear
The breeze was short-lived
No ripples stir
the surface now

Another world is there
a world of muted greens and
browns
and sable black
Of dancing ferns
more delicate than lace
Cobwebby
transluscent

Rushes
tall and stately
guard the river
spiking the sky
Grasses trail slim fingers
in the cool water

'A penny for them, friend,'
A voice explains

Gone the river
Gone the green rushes

A 'penny'
he said!

Dolly Sewell

CHATTERING CHARTERIS OF EARL STERNDALE

She stood beside the pillarbox
Chateris the chatterbox
Telling tales and prattling
Idle talk and nattering
Her tongue a tittle-tattling
To spread the common word.

Of secrets and solicitudes
And shibby-shabby attitudes
Of sinners sinful escapades
And certain folks uncertain trades
All the gossip was relayed
And told as she heard.

For Charteris the chatterbox
Was nothing but a natterbox
A windbag of the wicked kind
Gossip-mongering on her mind
So eagerly she'd seek and find
A problem to be shared.

The vicar or the village fool
Mistress of the village school
Were tainted by her jabberling
And hounded by her babbling
Were haunted by her gabbling
For nobody was spared.

At home within her tidy house
She niggled hourly at her spouse
Night and day it never stopped
Until her head he cruelly chopped
From body to the ground it dropped
And lay there quite absurd.

The quiet woman she became
Was never known to speak again
And so a lesson let it be
To those who chatter idly
A wise man does it quietly
And lives to spread the word.

Patricia P. Jones

ALPORT HEIGHT

From this cold wind spot
on a late, weekday afternoon
when the Height is deserted
I play God,
focus the flywheel,
skim to distant houses
and hold an entire village within one bloomed lens.

While the wind carries rooks in higher flight
the far horizon shadows and clarifies
with embryonic storms —
slate grey and topaz —
and I watch you picking harebells
to take a memory home.

Jeremy Duffield

ON MIDDLETON EDGE

If this life-saving rock should fail
Yielding too much to my embrace
And rock and I to death should race,
The rock would stay there in the dale
While I, breaking my fall,
Would still go on
Farther than any wandering star has gone.

Andrew Young (1885-1971)

DERBYSHIRE LAPWINGS

What do they know of oceans
This score or more of moorlanders
Weaned on tarn water and cotton-bog?
What could they know of seas?

Yet, just now, as they banked together,
Line after line, piloting with one mind,
They flowed like ripplings of tide,
Licking and lipping at the shore.

Maybe the sea lies deep within them,
From their sanded feet, through to their crests,
The spume on their chests, the Sargossa greens
And Atlantic blacks in their backs,
The hiss of shingle, hiss of waves
Swishing in their outstretched wings.

The sea is all around them,
Carried whispering down threads of streams,
Held secretive and cupped in watery moorlines,
Hidden in the rise and falls of hills, wave upon wave,
Drifting in the sea rorque of timothy grass under winds,
Flung high in the rigging of hills beneath galleon clouds,
Beached in the marbled pebbles of their eggs.

All this mirrored in their purposed borrowing
Of the gull's tearful cry

Sea-wet, sea-wet

Giving everything away.

Roger Elkin

52

ARBOR LOW — STONE CIRCLE

Some other dream
silhouetted under Moon
and Northern star,
laid its haunting time
upon the sleeping stones,
undeciphered runes of whispers
drawn through silences.

Some other dream
distanced from our time,
caught the incense of moorland air
the pulse of summer,
fall of water from a distant crag
as green on gold, the tigering of day
streaked the white markers of antiquity.

Some other dream
woven in echoes,
like a litany
of souls,
hallows the timeless mystery
of the centre stone,
and waits through silences.

Doris Corti

ARBOR LOW

Here lies a circle of stones
too aged, too weary to stand upright.

Now resting on the verge of mounds
they've stumbled, like exhausted climbers,
overlooking boundaries of stone-walling
circuiting farms and smallholdings.

Then, high above, a lark, an unseen —
singing — centrifugal voice urges all
to rise and be counted — before
another quake, another Armageddon
changes the landscape.

Arda Lacey

FLASH DAM

Flash Dam is large, emphatic.
Its water touches tarmac,
The sky falls silent in it.
No swans pleat the stretch, cleave
Or reveal how really deep.

Thirty years ago this pond
Took a boy from his tipped boat,
Drew him screaming through the clear
Certainty of tons of death,
Graveweight on him till he drowned.

The engine in the blank house
Fanned waves into tame water
For hot baths down in the town.
The road blackened a little
From the excitement, litter
Dribbled inwards. The boat rocked
To the side, the dam relaxed.

To-day it will let you froth
Its shallows with your hand.
Toy cars out for a day's run
Can circle it with no sound
As your fingers swim or drown.

Patrick Hare

THOMAS BRINDLEY'S GRAVE
IN BRADBOURNE CHURCHYARD

It is quiet,
though the wind is strong
and the light darkening,
and here the Buxton's lie
and Eyres,
and others in tilted graves
with headstones lichened to obscurity,
noted names,
with a brief epitaph
to catch and hold the eye a moment longer;
but in what quiet, undisclosed corner
does Thomas Brindley's unmarked grave
shroud his paupers bones?

In the long grass
no mound arrests the gaze,
and only the stone faces
thrusting from the ancient tower
still remain as witness to that scene
of mournful interment.
And of his life?
The Bradbourne Parish Register;
the accounts by Overseers of the poor;
and the damning '51 Census —
Thomas Brindley — pauper:
an illiterate
who worked the fields
and slept on straw,
who stood each Michaelmas
proving he had the strength to work,
and who was loved by a wife
who bore his daughter Ellen
whose great-great-grandson
now stands and feels the ground chill
and the breeze thrill the hairs upon his neck.

Jeremy Duffield

WELL DRESSINGS

Water, celebrated for its life giving power:
Villagers create a religious scene,
A shrine of flowers and ferns.
Clay, softened by the eager hands and feet of children
and salted to prevent drying out.
Mixture spread smooth into wooden trays
and pattern pricked out with artistic flair,
of animals, people and birds.
Colourless shapes,
embroidered with blossom and evergreen,
spring to life.

Jean Fairclough

A CONTINUITY OF HANDS

This year she sits and watches
the dressing of her well.

As a child she'd loved
the yellowness of buttercups
and picked some for the picture's sun;
rejected as they wouldn't last
she'd bunched them in a jar at home.

Armfuls of bluebells made a lovely sky,
a misty mauvy-blue eternity.
Her daughter has hydrangeas now
petalling the sky with frown of clouds.

Men carted boards
to soak in the village pond;
took time off from the farm to collect clay
and puddle it, a background for the flowers.
She chuckled, remembering her grandson's muddy face,
clothes and wellies when he tried to help.

The thrill of being allowed to have a part.
How her young fingers ached
in spelling out the headboard
JOSEPH'S SPECIAL COAT
in rhododendron buds.
Later she helped with the picture,
fixing pebbles, lichen, moss.

Progressing to designer,
she chose THE SERMON ON THE MOUNT,
using her husband's hair for Jesus' beard;
tried eggshell for the faces
and they became so very much alive.

She watches her family's skilled hands
create WE PLOUGH THE FIELDS AND SCATTER:
looks forward to the blessing of her well.

Fay Eagle

VERSES HUNG ON THE MANTELSHELF
AT THE ISAAC WALTON INN, DOVEDALE.

Lord give me grace that even I
May catch so fine and fat a fish
That there will be no need to lie
To gratify my wildest wish.

Hullo, what's this, what's this;
No wish to lie about a fish?
Why man 'twould spoil 'bout half the sport
To give no more than true report.

Anon

from **THE RETIREMENT**
(stanzas to Izaak Walton)

Oh my beloved Nymph! fair Dove,
Princess of rivers, how I love
    Upon thy flow'ry Banks to lie,
        And view thy Silver stream,
When gilded by a Summer's Beam!
And in it, all thy wanton Fry
        Playing at liberty,
And with my Angle upon them
    The All of treachery
I ever lean'd to practise and to try!

Charles Cotton

IN DOVEDALE

Isaac! still thou anglest near me
By the green banks of thy Dove,
Still thy gentle ghost may hear me
Breathe my reverence and love.

Thou, whose ears drank in the warble
Of all streams in crystal play, —
Will thy bones beneath cold marble
Lie in peace so far away?

O my kindly old piscator,
See'st thou not these waters clear?
Time, thou changeling, Time, thou traitor,
Give him back, — his home was here!

Lo! at yonder bend he standeth,
Where round rocks the wave bells out,
See! with skilful touch he landeth
Now a grayling, now a trout.

Stream of beauty! winding, singing
Through the world's divinest dale,
Ever to thy music bringing
That old spirit calm and pale!

Learned in all honest learning,
Trustful, truthful, pure of heart;
Peaceful, blameless honour earning
By the magic of his art.

In life's fitful turmoil often
Have I longed to be like him,
And have felt my nature soften
Musing on that phantom dim, —

Now a trout and now a grayling
Luring from the shaded pool,
God's white clouds high o'er him sailing,
All around the beautiful!

Henry Glassford Bell (1803-1874)

SHE DWELT AMONG THE UNTRODDEN WAYS

She dwelt among the untrodden ways
Beside the springs of Dove,
A Maid whom there were none to praise
And very few to love:

A violet by a mossy stone
Half hidden from the eye!
— Fair as a star, when only one
Is shining in the sky.

She lived unknown, and few could know
When Lucy ceased to be;
But she is in her grave, and, oh,
The difference to me!

William Wordsworth (1770-1850)

DERBYSHIRE

The river Dove flows down its Dale
And ripples just as sweetly
As when good Master Walton hied
With Master Cotton by his side,
To angle there completely.

And sometimes Master Walton scored,
And sometimes Master Cotton;
But sometimes neither caught a fish,
When Isaak sadly murmured "Pish!"
And Charles said roundly, "Rotten!"

E. V. Lucas (1868-1938)

from DOVEDALE ON A SPRING DAY

Approach we then this classic ground;
More gentle name was never found
By chance, nor more of picturing sound
To tell the spirit of the scene;
Be Dovedale ours this April day,
This April day that sheen or gray
May whip the wavelets into spray
Or flood with sun the margent green.

For all that wild work on the height
And driven clouds hailstone-gray, and fight
Of venturers on the ridge, delight
Is April's way and Dovedale's mind;
These chasms and spikes that might elsewhere
Be monsters, horror's host, despair
In effigy, through this favouring air
Are hanging silks with dreams designed.

From those rich kingcups at the foot
Of soaring rock whence yew trees shoot
Up to the flashing swift pursuit
Of cloud on cloud where stone cuts sky,
It might be peril's deadliest hold;
The wheeling rooks are much too bold,
To build there? but the trees unfold
In tenderest green a sweet reply.

And see this stream that marches strong
With urgent and invincible song,
In myriad spearheads hurled along,
Assailing, sallying, arrowing miles;
Immensely as his lordship roars,
He rides but into Oberon's wars,
Forget-me-not from both his shores
Watches his wrath with blue-eyed smiles ...

From abbot's-kitchen caves aloft
(I thought none lived there) cobweb-soft
A mystery grows, the winds up-waft
The smoke of an enchanter's fire;
But that enchanter proves no more
Than the boys' fancy who explore
His threshold, study and corridor,
And gnome-like dart about his spire.

We here in grace have gladly passed
Beyond the world, behind us cast
Its tumult; for that Titan blast
Which makes the cawing rooks unheard
Is this dream's own, and we float on
In dream-time, love and nature one,
Hand folding hand, as flower and sun,
And wave and stone, and song and word.

Edmund Blunden (1896-1944)

DOVEDALE DAWN

Grass scrunches beneath my feet
as pale light creeps into dark.
In the day's first breath
stepping stones waver and dissolve
where silver tongues of water lap,
moulding a ribbon of molten metal.

The dog snuffles undergrowth
scatters birds towards fading stars.
Sun tips the horizon
gilds ghost grey trees,
evaporates breath
in a burst of warmth.

Somewhere, a gritstone's lorry grinds,
crashes silence,
turns night to day.

Barbara Horrocks

SHROVETIDE FOOTBALL AT ASHBOURNE

Once a year Ashbourne returns to Olde England,
This pleasant country town becomes bedecked
with rough boards, shutters, barricades.
Vestiges of civilisation remain of course,
policemen patrol in rough farm boots.
Then the National Anthem, the ceremonial 'throwing-up'
But pubs have reverted to ale-houses,
back to a time before closing-time.
Roaring mobs roam the little streets
in sinister ragged clothes and heavy boots.
But — inside their warriors' clothes,
hiding behind the beer-stoked faces
are respectable family men, farmers,
students, Rotary Club members —
All having a day off.
In the fearsome sprawling 'hug'.
Inside the gut-wrenching sweating mob,
look carefully and you'll detect
a smile across a face or two.
For they've quietly slipped away again
from civilisation's gentle grasp ...
for yet another year.

Les Baynton

FOOTBALL AT ASHBOURNE ON SHROVE TUESDAY

Up'ards and Down'ards
Unders and overs
Bakers and butchers
And cobblers and drovers
Farmers and farriers
And fiddlers all
Dribbling and kicking
And clouting a ball.

North'ners and South'ners
Catchers and keepers
Coopers and carters
And gardeners and 'sweepers
Groomsmen and herdsmen
And furriers four
All pushing and pulling
And trying to score.

Football at Ashbourne
Played through the town
In back streets, in alleys
And all the way down
To Henmores' flush waters
The game rushes on
Splishing and splashing
Go father and son.

The ball's weighing heavy
Filled full of cork dust
Men stagger and swagger
It's mill wheels or bust
To Sturston, to Clifton
With goal posts in sight
Right lads, it's now lads
Aim, shoot and strike.

Patricia P Jones

SIR BROOKE BOOTHBY
(after the painting by Joseph Wright of Derby, 1781)

Sir Brooke, reclining by a brook,
How punningly your lines flow
Beside your namesake. Time has changed
The leaves to autumn overhead.
You clasp Rousseau.

And all your nature's heraldry
Is here set out. It is your look —
Voluptuous, thoughtful, quizzical, —
Has puzzled me for many years,
Belov'd Sir Brooke.

Two years ago they cleaned you up.
Still sensuous, you leer the less,
No longer the seducer but
Hinting of sorrows yet to come,
And pensiveness.

Yet still amused, — you scrutinise
Me as intently as I you.
Dumpy and old, I've fared the worse.
Will others come when I am gone,
Or be as true?

My very sparkling Brooke, we are
Two centuries and Styx apart.
Yet mirror-imaged our loss
(Your child, my father) and we share
A love for art.

It would be pleasant if we were
Among the leaves so juxtaposed
You on the left, I on the right
That you would flow above me when
The book was closed.

Gerda Mayer

NIGHT MOORING ON THE EREWASH CANAL

A vixen barks: wind freshens:
overhead
the Plough is bright and steady.

The boat creaks at its mooring pin.
Water's
a shining rope to the next lock.

Geese honk. Cropped trees scratch
the glowing skirt
of the twinkling sky.

One bright star rays a halo
like
a child's drawing of a simple sun.

From right to left, a long woosh
of Intercity
stretches out the dark.

Stars roar their brightness but
I cannot hear
their shout. Their light is silence.

Inside my head a song warms.
Is identified.
Contentment threatens.

Let my ears prick remembrance
and fingers
scribe before the itch is smothered.

Maggie Norton

from THE ECONOMY OF VEGETATION

Nymphs!whose fair eyes with vivid lustres glow
For human weal, and melt at human wo;
Late as you floated on your silver shells,
Sorrowing and slow by Derwent's willowy dells;
Where by tall groves his foamy flood he steers
Through ponderous arches o'er impetuous wears,
By Derby's shadowy towers reflective sweeps,
And gothic grandeur chills his dusky deeps;
You pearl'd with pity's drops his velvet sides,
Sigh'd in his gales, and murmur'd in his tides,
Waved o'er his fringed brink a deeper gloom,
And bow'd his alders o'er Milcena's tomb.

Erasmus Darwin (1731-1802)

PORCELAIN

Fragile paste is formed
into figurines,
objects of artistic perfection;
crowned symbols of Derby.
Clay is gracefully turned
into effortless shapes,
glaze applied —
then by a miracle
fired into new creation.

Linda S. Hardy

A WALK THROUGH TIME

Trampled by the feet of Danes, Romans, Saxon and Bronze Ages
remnants of their passing in stone and Doomsday Book pages.
All Saints Church parades its two hundred foot tower
and successive Earls of Derby were the ministers of power.
We take a jump across time to the industrial revolution
where famous names sought to find their own solutions.

Fresh life came to Derby via its waterways and locks
transport for industries from textiles to locomotive stock
The Lombard Silk Mill drew power from the swift Derwent race
industries thrived, making silk, hosiery, cotton and lace.
In 1875 William Duesbury's china was approved by Royal Seal
painted figurines and flowers enhancing the porcelain's feel.

Derby grew as railway lines merged, faster became the pace
steel mills, boiler plants and aero engines joined the race.
New industries of railway plants and modern engineering
and Rolls Royce was founded by adventurous pioneering.
Old family businesses graced each lane and narrow street
buildings of character, oak doors; stone steps worn by feet.

Now we have huge indoor markets with sheltering glass domes
displaying clothes, antiques and hand made ice cream cones.
Some streets are gone now beneath cobbled pedestrian walks
with tables laid in the sun to encourage friendly talks.
Tall signs direct visitors to heritage museums and sights
the cascading white waterfalls our newest delight.

The Derby Ram presides in majestic glory over East Street
on the cross road junction where Albion Street meets.
As a new century approaches plans are being eagerly hatched
for new buildings and new ideas; a far cry from the past.

Marjorie Anne Finney

DERBY'S CROWN

What makes a city behave like a city
instead of a large market town?
Where is the part that's known as the heart
and what does she wear for a crown?

"She's a town not a city!" officialdom screamed
And Irongate noted the snubs
As most of the prayers breathed in Amen Alley
Found their way to the local pubs.

Derby's folklore cursed friends of Charles the first
who, they said, had it in for the Tup
After Nottingham's standard supported the crown
and Derby kept her flag rolled up.

"Her population's not big enough!"
cried the man in the three cornered hat.
Said the Tup, "Rolls and Royce aren't that small,
Joe Wright's rather tall; and not one of the Rams is a sprat."

The town centre sang and the football ground rang
When the honour at last was bestowed
Despite the delay, the tups to this day
swear the cock on the Corn Market crowed.

Cockpit Hill and Canal Tavern
Made way for the Eagle's feet
A city indeed, but Derby's need
Was still a place where old friends could meet.

The city's pulse beats in her modernised streets
The Royal Crown Derby's her gem.
But her heart's in the part where the markets still meet
And her sons are her diadem.

Doreen Chapman

LINKED BY LAMPLIGHT

They both are found upon a plinth —
Silent as a shadow's ghost;
He stands on the Company's soil
And she where sickness forms a host.

Scutari back to Holloway —
She should have had a regal car;
She who saved so many men
And still shines like the brightest star.

He lit the Cities' sprawling streets
And helped to make the roaring gun —
Worked on the rail then on the road
To give a peaceful silent run.

And was it chance or was it planned
That his first Derby works should be
Along a road whose name evokes
A thoroughbred tenacity?

So he, precision's engineer —
The one who made perfection's car —
Might travel back for further toil
At night; designers' brightest star;

And nearing there, this man named Royce,
Might give one of his men a hail,
And in his headlamp's beam he'd see
The road's charmed name — Nightingale.

Richard Acton

LONER IN THE MORNING

The clouds of early
morning lay low with rain.
I climbed upon my bike
in starched overalls,
looking for my friend,
and riding free.
Through Derby Town all
hell came down below
the clouds.

Black, evil, wings ripping,
guns flashing, bombs falling,
a plane, unaware
that children were below,
dispensed its filthy metal.
Hawthorne Street, Rolls
Royce, were now aglow,
Mothers screamed as
bodies splattered.

There are no boundaries
when bullets fly,
people cry, sometimes die.

Hell has passed
and left its carnage.

On a landscape
now in fear,
I lay on tarmac
riveted with steel.
Bike destroyed,
body bleeding,
some lay dead and
some lay moaning
in the early morning mist.

No school today,
No work today.
War has struck
into the world
of innocents, and
 slain them.

Our overalls now used
like shrouds,
I stood bleeding.

D. H. Griffiths

TO MRS. GARNETT
HOUSEKEEPER AT KEDLESTONE HALL 1776 — 1809

"a most distinct Articulator."
Samuel Johnson

What could you tell me if alive today?
Your half-length portrait is hanging belowstairs.
You stand upright, small, elderly, aristocratic nose
and eyes that seem to pierce my own.
A tall black velvet bonnet gives you height.
You wear your best silk dress and white-bowed blouse.
The background's plain, no pillars, urns,
lush drapery, to take attention from your vivid face.
The printed catalogue of pictures, statues, furnishings
lies open, held in black-gloved hand.
Your task, his lordship is away in town,
to guide the visitors of classic taste around his country home.

Imagine Johnson, Boswell arriving in a chaise;
the parkland seems so natural — in fact was planned by man,
the village cleared away, replaced by lakes and trees.
A footman hands them down; they climb
the sweeping flight of steps. You are the mistress of the house,
conduct your own Grand Tour through marble hall
in which a Roman senator would feel at home;
sarcophagus-shaped seats, Homeric frieze and niches
holding casts of goddesses and gods.
"Just right for an assize court" Johnson said.

You take them through the music room, withdrawing room
and library where Adam's books on architecture
including his designs for Kedlestone,
and Johnson's dictionary are chosen for display.
Large paintings, biblical and pagan are inset on the walls
and in the dining room stark pictures of dead game.

As I wander, National Trust guide in hand
you seem to walk beside me — a homely touch
in this Augustan house.

Fay Eagle

TO THE IMPRISONED QUEEN AT WINGFIELD

I have wasted too much time in reading
while the summer evening darkens into night.
Purple fingers of vermilion sky
carry the quiet stillness
and night's darkening shadows shadow darker
this vaulted crypt.
Cramped, I stand,
and climb the curving steps up to the hall.

Where fires blazed now last year's leaves still lie
and bats, from hidden crevices,
cry piping through the empty passages of time
where Tudor music plays in weathered stone.
I trace the outline of your room —
your windows dark silhouette.

Come, descend Mary, take my hand
and join the courtyard dance.
Your love outlives these lichened rooms and towers
and the soft kiss you blew into the night
falls soft around me still,
while in this ageless darkness I await
your returning love.

Jeremy Duffield

SOUTH WINGFIELD MANOR

High across the fields
it wavers through the mists
like the smudged strokes
of a child's paint brush;
grey on grey, dark against light,
chimneys, high tower, gable end.

All ruin now
no warmth or comfort;
the past is roofless,
cold hearths and vacant windows,
fireplaces stacked up —
The North wind blasts the walls
the cracks widen and the cold
roars in.

A less than savoury prison for a Queen.
Mary sickened, grey with waiting,
smiled only for her gypsy;
Babington, half in love with royalty
and half with romance;
The foolish plots foredoomed.

We have come on a Winter day
no violets or celandines.
A scatter of snowdrops
drift under the North wall,
a flutter of white flakes
melt into the shining wet stones.

It is a kind of pilgrimage.

Berenice Moore

CRICH TRAMS

Ten tons of wood and steel for just ten pounds,
the price to pay to stay the breaker's hand.
Our city streets no longer ring with sounds
of wheel on rail, for buses rule the land.

Bright painted tramcars, no more to be seen
in English towns, climb high through Derby hills.
The grime where once they worked replaced by green,
the worker's transport gives the tourist thrills.

Malcolm Chisholm

MY FIRST VISIT TO CRICH TRAM MUSEUM

I feel like a child at a funfair,
The hoardings just tear me apart.
My heart skips a beat
On the old cobbled street,
And TRAMS going backwards are SMART!

Brenda Courtie

A CROMFORD PIECE

Arkwright might well be surprised to learn his
Cradle of the Industrial Revolution that
Rocked him to fame while children tumbled,
Over-tired, to early graves and exhausted
Men and women sweated in the deafening clangs
From water-frame and spinning-jenny has
Outlived two hundred years and still stands,
Redoubt-like, behind its towering walls.
Doubtless, though, he wouldn't begin to understand how
Politics have fashioned Cromford's decline to sideline his
Inventive skills till his mill's reduced to
Exhibition space, silent rooms, or rash of shops where
Coach-loads of folk pick over imported clothes made
Even cheaper in the sweatier shops of the Far East.

Roger Elkin

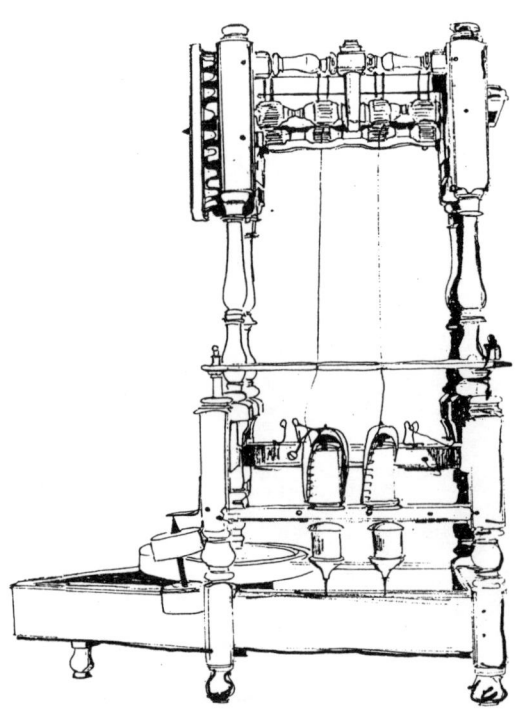

DERBY TO MATLOCK

Derby, church spires
and open farmland, wide pastures,
passing through hillside villages
and red-brick chimneys.
To Duffield,
with its Georgian
and Victorian houses
and dark stone farm buildings
bordering the track.
The River Derwent,
filled with tall marsh-reeds,
passes through thick sloping forests,
deepest of green-grass valleys,
and bracken-covered stone
to Ambergate, Whatstandwell
and hillside towns and farms.
To Matlock Bath's sheer-faced escarpment —
cable cars leading to
the Heights of Abraham.
Deep tunnel opens
to views of Riber Castle,
high across the Derwent valley
from Matlock.

Francia Turner

MATLOCK BATH

From Matlock Bath's half-timbered station
I see the black dissenting spire —
Thin witness of a congregation,
Stone emblems on a Handel choir;
In blest Bethesda's limpid pool
Comes treacling out of Sunday School.

By cool Siloam's shady rill —
The sounds are sweet as strawberry jam:
I raise mine eyes unto the hill,
the beetling HEIGHTS OF ABRAHAM;
The branchy trees are white with rime
In Matlock Bath this winter-time,

And from the whiteness, grey uprearing,
Huge cliffs hang sunless ere they fall,
A tossed and stony ocean nearing
The moment to o'erwhelm us all:
Eternal Father, strong to save,
How long wilt thou suspend the wave?

How long before the pleasant acres
Of interesting LOVERS' WALKS
Are rolled across by limestone breakers,
Whole woodlands snapp'd like cabbage stalks?
O God, our help in ages past,
How long will SPEEDWELL CAVERN last?

In this dark dale I hear the thunder
Of houses folding with the shocks,
The GRAND PAVILION buckling under
The weight of the ROMANTIC ROCKS,
The hardest Blue-John ash-trays seem
To melt away in thermal steam.

Deep in their Nonconformist setting
The shivering children wait their doom —
The father's whip, the mother's petting
In many a coffee-coloured room;
And attic bedrooms shriek with fright,
For dread of Pilgrims of the Night.

Perhaps it's this that makes me shiver
As I ascend the slippery path
High, high above the sliding river
And terraces of Matlock Bath:
A sense of doom, a dread to see
The rock of Ages cleft for me.

Sir John Betjeman (1906-1984)

A LIGHT REPORT ON MATLOCK BATH

I walk along the promenade,
Guest houses smell of toast:
Chip shops and amusement sites,
It's just like at the coast.

With sixty thousand coloured bulbs,
The sight just makes me quiver
As they display their vivid light
Reflecting on the river.

An aurora borealis
That never seems to cease
Glistens on the water
And on Canadian geese.

There's a multitude of things to do,
Like medieval fights,
and watching the embellished boats
on the Venetian nights.

The adornment of this spectacle
Gives a feeling of euphoria:
And all is absolutely free
Courtesy of Queen Victoria.

Len Chesters

TO D. H. LAWRENCE

You, who all your life
were crossing borders,
whose 'come-from' included
a grandfather's Derbyshire roots,
freewheeled in youth, cycling
from Eastwood down to the Erewash,
climbed the darker-than-limestone tors
of Matlock, marvelling at crinoids, finding
fresh perspectives in space and time.
You walked in woodland of sessile oak,
one with the life of its creatures, yet
aware of black cloisters nearby, smelling
the coaldust which choked your father.

Sure of a new world within, travelling
beyond the country of your heart,
you could not have foreseen
your permanent arrival in the sun —
bright mountains above Taos,
heights over the Rio Grande,
among hibiscus flowers, blue balsam pines —
Kiowa Ranch where Frieda settled
your ashes, carried across continents
(deathmask made at Vence), to be
forever part of England in a foreign pasture.
Mexico, a long way from Matlock.

Gladys Mary Coles

DERBYSHIRE SONG

Come loving me to Darley Dale
In spring time or sickle time,
And we will make as proud a tale
As lovers in the antique prime
Of Harry or Elizabeth.

With kirtle green and nodding flowers
To deck my hair and little waist,
I'll be worth a lover's hours ...
Come, fellow, thrive, there is no haste
But soon is worn away in death.

Soon shall the blood be tame, and soon
Our bodies lie in Darley Dale,
Unreckoning of jolly June,
With tongues past telling any tale;
My man, come loving me today.

I have a wrist is smooth and brown,
I have a shoulder smooth and white,
I have my grace in any gown
By sun or moon or candle-light ...
Come Darley way, come Darley way.

John Drinkwater (1882-1937)

T'BARMOTE COURT WILL PUT THINGS RIGHT

When mining men laid down their tools
And sat by fireside bright,
They talked of work and soughs and lead
And t'Barmote Court of right.

Their pipes were smoked and ale was supped,
Talk drifted round and round,
Of heavy strikes and poor returns,
And trouble over ground.

The search for lead (and minerals)
Was hard and rough and tough,
To work a mine or drive a shaft
To make a drainage sough.

And Kingsfield land until this day
Has special powers of right,
But should some landlord hold them back
T'Barmote Court will put it right.

For on this land by royal decree,
No let or hindrance laid
Must stop the honest miner
From toiling at his trade.

Seven-hundred years, or more
Passed since this court was found,
To settle disputes far and wide
On all the mining ground.

Twelve good men and true, they say,
Examine every plight.
The body of the mine are they,
t'Barmote Court puts all things right.

Ken Westhead

COLLIERY ROW — BLACKWELL 1955.

It was the last call on a Friday night —
I was ten
and helped my dad hawk meat
from the back of a green Austin van.

In Blackwell — on Primrose Hill or The Ridge —
I ran up entries with my enamel tray
or knocked on doors and shouted 'Butcher'

— but not in Colliery Row.

Here the terraced houses stepped the cobbled street,
paint peeled off doors
cardboard mended windows
and tin baths hung on outside walls;
smoke and blackness,
netted windows hung with filth
scared me.

The colliery was below —
lights
and smoke and steam
and the whirling of the winding wheel
hypnotic —
but black and brooding.

Men squatted by fallen brick walls,
their women leaned in doorways
— thin armed, hard-faced
or with big bosoms and frocks
that reached only to their knees.

All noise:
swearing and yelling —
the dogs always barking ...
and the black-faced kids rattled the van doors,
pressed snotty noses to the window glass,
spat
and jeered — wanting to fight.

In Colliery Row I was always afraid —
for myself
and for my dad who had to serve;

and the only time I left the van
was to talk to a girl my age
who was crying
in the street
wearing only a dirty vest.

Jeremy Duffield

BETRAYAL

Creswell has known better times.
A large village with forty shops
— never elegant or chocolate boxy —
has become a ghost town.
     The pit has closed.

Once-proud men gather on street corners
and the hurt shows.
Unused to idleness, without the price of a pint,
they feel ashamed,
as if it's their fault,
Boot fairs replace Big Band nights
     And the slags grow green.

Joy St. Clair

EPITAPH ON BESS OF HARDWICK

Four times the nuptial bed she warmed,
And every time so well performed,
That when death spoiled each husband's billing,
He left the widow every shilling.
Fond was the dame, but not dejected;
Five stately mansions she erected
With more than royal pomp, to vary
The prison of her captive Mary.
When Hardwick's towers shall bow their head,
Nor mass be more in Worksop said;
When Bolsover's fair fame shall tend,
Like Oldcotes, to its mouldering end;
When Chatsworth tastes no Cavendish bounties,
Let fame forget this costly countess.

Horace Walpole (1717-1797)

CROOKED SPIRE, CHESTERFIELD

Between Derby and Sheffield,
Chesterfield comes into view,
with its twisted
contorted landmark.
A spire
beguiling the eye,
defying the laws
of structural engineering.
One of England's wonders,
riveting our attention
as we pass from close
Derbyshire hills,
through a town inspired by
its Leaning Tower of the North.

Francia Turner

MOB'S CAP

A strange rock pile on Millstone Edge in Derbyshire

A million years
Have passed this stone,
Weathered by the elemental force;
Mob's Cap
Queen's it on the ridge —
A monolith to unrelenting time.

Quietly she sat
And watched men toil and strain,
To build their fort of stone and flint;
Unnamed battles
She has seen
Of unknown, prehistoric man.

Stone cutters came,
Their hammers ringing clear,
Till giant stones were rolled away
To waiting millers
With golden grain,
To pulverise to fine brown dust.

Indifferent rock
Calmly sits and waits
For time and history to change.
The walker
Passes by
Untroubled by stone calendars.

Stan Smith

LITTLE JOHN OF HATHERSAGE

He has lain undisturbed
in St. Michael's churchyard
these long centuries
since his best adventures
with Robin Hood;
both were well outlawed
at the defeat of their leader,
Simon de Montfort.

The earl had revolted
against the fiscal imposts
of King Henry III,
an absentee tax-gatherer
who exported the tolls
to European foundations,
ruling England from Rome
or Paris; rarely from home.

John's powerful bow,
which this giant carried
into the Battle of Evesham,
once framed the church nave;
less bellicose echoes
can be raised over ale
in *The Scotsman's Pack*
downhill from the grave.

J. D. Mallinson

AN ANCIENT RHYME

respecting Welbeck Abbey, Hardwick Hall, Bolsover Castle and Worksop Manor. Written c.1620 by a Dr. Andrewes. (Quoted at end of Lady Ottoline Morrell's Early Memoirs)

Hardwicke for hugeness, Worsope for height,
Welbeke for use, and Bolser for sighte;
Worsope for walks, Hardwicke for hall,
Welbecke for brewhouse, Bolser for all.
Welbecke a parish, Hardwicke a court,
Worsope a pallas, Bolser a fort;
Bolser to feast, Welbecke to ride in,
Hardwicke to thrive, and Worsope to hide in.
Hardwicke good house, Welbecke good keepinge,
Worsope good walkes, Bolser good sleepinge;
Bolser new built, Welbecke well mended,
Hardwicke concealed, and Worsope extended.
Bolser is morn, Welbecke day bright,
Hardwicke high noone, Worsope good night;
Hardwicke is now, and Welbecke will last,
Bolser will be, and Worsope is past,
Wellbecke a wife, Bolser a maide,
Hardwicke a matron, Worsope decaide;
Worsope is wise, Welbecke is wittie,
Hardwicke is hard, Bolser is prettie.
Hardwicke is rich, Welbecke is fine,
Warsope is statelie, Bolser divine;
Hardwicke a chest, Welbecke a saddle,
Worsope a throne, Bolser a cradle.
Hardwicke resembles Hampton Court much,
And Worsope Windsor, Bolser Nonesuch;
Worsope a duke, Hardwicke an earl,
Welbecke a viscount, Bolser a pearl.
The rest are jewels of the sheere,
Bolser the pendant of the eare.

Dr. Andrewes

ACKNOWLEDGEMENTS

For use of copyright material grateful acknowlegement is made to:
Edward Boaden Thomas for 'Seven Wonders' from *The Twelve Parts of Derbyshire* (Derbyshire County Council, 1988). Judith Thwaite for 'BC' from *Clapping in the Wings* (National Poetry Foundation, 1996). Brian Blackwell for 'Monuments to Unknown Men', first published by The Salopian Society (1995). Mary Brett for 'White Peak Spring' from *Low Tide* (National Poetry Foundation, 1995). Peggy Poole for 'Dry Stone Walls' from *Cherry Stones and Other Poems* (Headland, 1983); and 'The 200th Victim' from *No Wilderness in Them* (Windows, 1984). Margaret Caunt for 'Winnats Pass' from *No-One About* (National Poetry Foundation, 1993). The Estate of John Drinkwater for 'Millers Dale' and 'Derbyshire Song' from *Collected Poems of John Drinkwater, Vol.1* (Sidgwick & Jackson, 1923). Myra Schneider for 'Millers Dale' first published in *Smiths Knoll*, 1993. Wendy Bardsley for 'Mr Willoughby's Kiss' from *Steel Wings* (Headland, 1998). Mary Hodgson for 'Mrs Hancock's Dilemma in a Theological Age' first published in *Pennine Platform*, 1993. Susan Skinner for 'The Rock' from *The Minnow Catching Boys* (Headland, 1995). Jean Stanbury for 'Bakewell Pudding' from *Winged Seeds* (National Poetry Foundation, 1997). Doris Corti for 'Arbor Low Stone Circle', first published in *The Unsaid Goodnight* (Stride, 1989). The Estate of Andrew Young for 'On Middleton Edge' from *Poems of Our Time* Dent 1945. Patricia P. Jones for 'Chattering Charteris of Earl Sterndale' and 'Football at Ashbourne on Shrove Tuesday' from *Tradition Magazine*, 1995 & 1996. Berenice Moore for 'Through Dark Doors' first published in *Tees Valley Writer*, 1991. Pat Moneypenny for 'Haddon Hall' from *Flames of Joy* 1982. Dolly Sewell for 'Lathkill Dale' first published in *The Field*. Jeremy Duffield for 'Alport Height' & 'Thomas Brindley's Grave in Bradourne Churchyard' from *Danced by the Light of the Moon* 1995, and 'To the Imprisoned Queen at Wingfield' from *Envoi Summer Anthology* 1989; and 'Colliery Row Blackwell 1955' from *Mining Poems* (Smith/ Doorstop, 1988). Patrick Hare for 'Flash Dam' from *Aeroplanes in Childhood* (Peterloo Poets, 1984). The Estate of E.V. Lucas for 'River Dove' from *Punch*, 18 April 1928. The Estate of Edmund Blunden for the extract from 'Dovedale on a Spring Day' from *A Book of Britain* compiled by John Hadfield (Hulton Press, 1956). Les Baynton for 'Shrovetide Football at Ashbourne' from *A Sense of Place* (East Midlands Arts, 1986). Gerda Mayer for 'Sir Brooke Boothby' from *With A Poet's Eye* (Tate Gallery Publications, 1986). Richard Acton for 'Linked by Lamplight' from *From Mining to the Swamps of Time* (Wayfarer's Press, 1994). Francia Turner for 'Derby to Matlock' and 'Crooked Spire, Chesterfield' from *Journeys* (David & Charles, 1989). The Estate of Sir John Betjeman and John Murray Ltd for 'Matlock Bath' from *Collected Poems of John Betjeman*

Special thanks are due to all the poets who have provided new work for the anthology. Every effort has been made to trace and contact copyright holders; any omission will be rectified on notification. Copyright remains with the authors.
92